A Note to P[arents]

DK READERS is a compelling program for beginning readers, designed in conjunction with leading literacy experts, including Dr. Linda Gambrell, Distinguished Professor of Education at Clemson University. Dr. Gambrell has served as President of the National Reading Conference, the College Reading Association, and the International Reading Association.

Beautiful illustrations and superb full-color photographs combine with engaging, easy-to-read stories to offer a fresh approach to each subject in the series. Each DK READER is guaranteed to capture a child's interest while developing his or her reading skills, general knowledge, and love of reading.

The five levels of DK READERS are aimed at different reading abilities, enabling you to choose the books that are exactly right for your child:

Pre-level 1: Learning to read
Level 1: Beginning to read
Level 2: Beginning to read alone
Level 3: Reading alone
Level 4: Proficient readers

The "normal" age at which a child begins to read can be anywhere from three to eight years old. Adult participation through the lower levels is very helpful for providing encouragement, discussing storylines, and sounding out unfamiliar words.

No matter which level you select, you can be sure that you are helping your child learn to read, then read to learn!

LONDON, NEW YORK, MUNICH,
MELBOURNE, and DELHI

Senior Editor Helen Murray
Senior Designer Robert Perry
Additional designers Owen Bennett,
Guy Harvey, and Rhys Thomas
Pre-Production Producer
Marc Staples
Producer Louise Minihane
Managing Editor Elizabeth Dowsett
Design Manager Ron Stobbart
Publishing Manager Julie Ferris
Art Director Lisa Lanzarini
Publishing Director Simon Beecroft

Reading Consultant Dr. Linda Gambrell

The LEGO© Movie screenplay by
Phil Lord and Christopher Miller

The LEGO© Movie story by
Dan Hageman & Kevin Hageman
and Phil Lord & Christopher Miller

Dorling Kindersley would like to thank Randi Sørensen
and Matthew James Ashton at the LEGO Group.

First American Edition, 2014
10 9 8 7 6 5 4 3 2 1
Published in the United States by DK Publishing
4th Floor, 345 Hudson Street, New York, New York 10014

001–193755–Jan/14

Page design copyright © 2014 Dorling Kindersley Limited

DK books are available at special discounts when purchased in bulk for sales
promotions, premiums, fund-raising, or educational use.
For details, contact: DK Publishing Special Markets, 4th Floor,
345 Hudson Street, New York, New York 10014
SpecialSales@dk.com

A catalog record for this book is available
from the Library of Congress.

ISBN: 978-1-4654-1695-7 (Paperback)
ISBN: 978-1-4654-1696-4 (Hardcover)

Color reproduction in the UK by Altaimage
Printed and bound in the USA by Lake Book Manufacturing, Inc.

Discover more at
www.dk.com
www.LEGO.com

Contents

DK READERS

BEGINNING TO READ ALONE 2

THE LEGO MOVIE

AWESOME ADVENTURES

HELEN MURRAY

Welcome to Bricksburg

The city of Bricksburg is a wonderful place to live. It is run by President Business, who rules the entire world.

A happy construction worker named Emmet lives in Bricksburg.

President Business

Emmet thinks President Business is a cool guy. Emmet and the people of Bricksburg love to follow President Business's instructions. They make sure everything runs just as he likes it.

Emmet

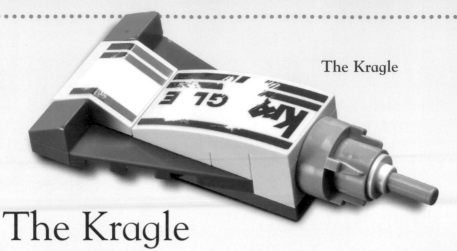

The Kragle

The Kragle

The Kragle is a mysterious object of great power. The mystical Vitruvius guarded the Kragle for many years.

One day, a controlling man named Lord Business stole the Kragle and blinded poor Vitruvius.

Vitruvius

Lord Business is actually President Business in disguise! He is going to use the Kragle to freeze the entire universe. Everything will stay just the way he wants it—forever!

Lord Business

The Special
Vitruvius predicted that somebody would rise up to defeat Lord Business. That person is called the Special.

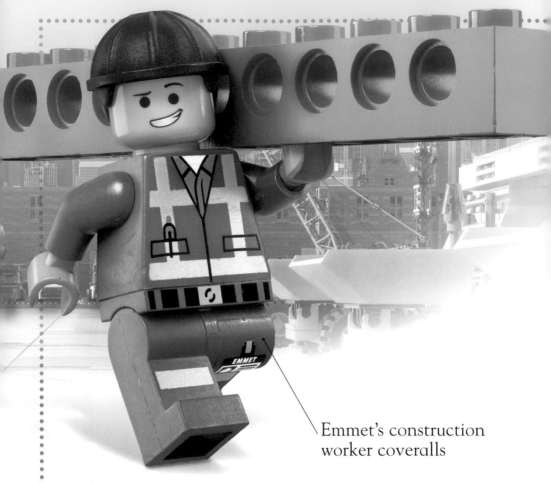

Emmet's construction worker coveralls

Emmet

Emmet enjoys his job on the Bricksburg construction site. He follows instructions carefully. He just wants to do a good job and to be liked by everyone.

One day,
Emmet's life takes
an extraordinary
turn when a
mysterious red
object gets stuck
to his back...

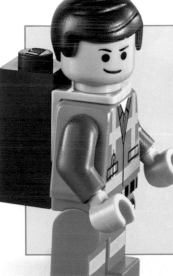

The Piece
The red object is called
the Piece of Resistance.
It is the only thing
that can stop Lord
Business's evil plans.
The person who finds
the Piece is the Special.

Super Secret Police

Watch out! Lord Business has a Super Secret Police force. He orders them to hunt down Emmet and the Piece.

Super Secret Police 4x4

The Super Secret
Police force is made
up of lots of
scary robots.
They are led
by Bad Cop.
He is not a robot.
He is just a very mean cop.
Bad Cop questions Emmet
about everything he knows.
Poor Emmet knows nothing!

Good Cop?

There are two sides to
Bad Cop: Bad Cop
and Good Cop.
Bad Cop seems to be
very much in control.

Good Cop

Bad Cop

"You're going to melt me?"

Emmet is chained up in the melting room by the Super Secret Police.

They have a terrifying giant laser machine and they are not afraid to use it!

Hang on! Who is that mysterious figure? It is a heroic Master Builder named Wyldstyle.

Chains

The robo police are no match for her speedy moves! She defeats the robots and frees Emmet.

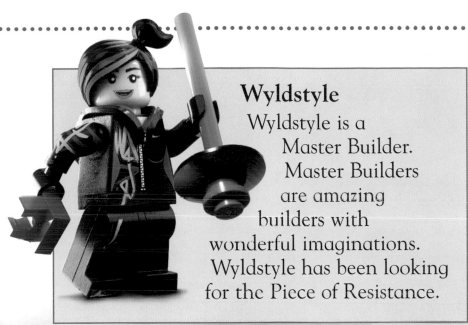

Wyldstyle

Wyldstyle is a Master Builder. Master Builders are amazing builders with wonderful imaginations. Wyldstyle has been looking for the Piece of Resistance.

The melting room

Laser beam

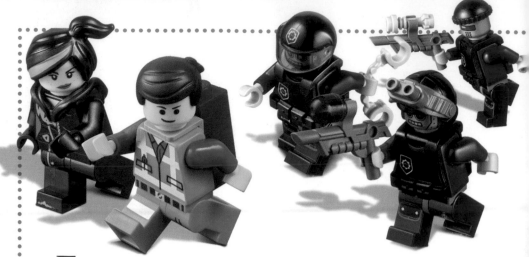

Epic escape

Emmet and Wyldstyle are chased by the robo police. Clever Wyldstyle creates an incredible Super Cycle out of pieces she finds in the alleyway.

Wyldstyle can build
anything out of anything.
Emmet thinks he is in love!
The pair zoom through
the city on the Super Cycle.
Next stop: the Wild West
to meet old Vitruvius.

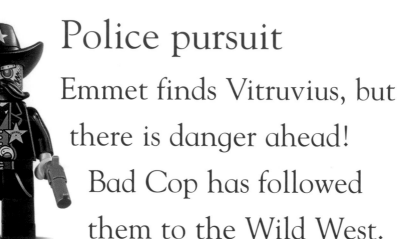

Police pursuit

Emmet finds Vitruvius, but there is danger ahead! Bad Cop has followed them to the Wild West. The cowboys are robots, too. They are all after Emmet!

Wyldstyle constructs a getaway glider to help them escape, but the heroes are not safe yet!

Bad Cop chases them in his speedy flying police car. There is no escape… until Batman swoops in to save them!

Batman

Batman is a Master Builder and Wyldstyle's boyfriend. He can build anything, as long as it is in black or very, very dark gray.

Cloud Cuckoo Land

The heroes travel up a rainbow to Cloud Cuckoo Land to meet the other Master Builders.

Unikitty

Cloud Cuckoo Land is the
happiest and most creative
place in the universe.
There are no rules here.
It is the home of Unikitty.
This adorable Master
Builder believes that all
ideas are good ideas,
except the not happy ones.

Angry Kitty
Unikitty tries to
stay positive all the
time, but sometimes
she snaps. She can
get very, very, very
VERY ANGRY!

Superman

Ghost

Artist

Abraham
Lincoln

Circus Clown

The Master Builders

Master Builders are the most
creative people in the universe.
They can build anything using
their incredible imaginations.
They are suprised to hear that
Emmet is the Special.
Emmet does not appear to
be brilliant or creative.
How will he stop Lord Business?

Panda Guy

Wonder Woman

El Macho

William Shakespeare

*To build...
or not to build!*

Marsha

Tracking device

Bad Cop has attached a tracking device to Emmet's leg.
The robo police have used it to follow him to Cloud Cuckoo Land!

Tracking device

A quick getaway

Emmet and his friends manage to escape the police—just barely! Two other heroic Master Builders also flee.

Benny is a Spaceman who loves building spaceships.

Benny

MetalBeard

MetalBeard is a pirate who lost most of his body parts in battle.

The Think Tank

All the other Master Builders
are taken to the Think Tank in
Lord Business's Office Tower.
He attaches them to a
machine to steal their ideas.
He wants to use their
creativity to make even
more evil plans.

The scary Office Tower

The heroes must break into Lord Business's Office Tower. Once inside, the Master Builders will free their friends and Emmet will put the Piece on the Kragle.

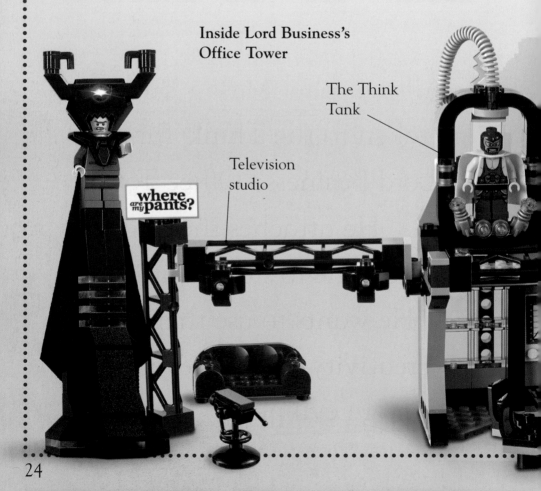

Inside Lord Business's Office Tower

The Think Tank

Television studio

where are my pants?

Emmet leads the gang inside.
They all work together to help
Emmet to sneak up
to the Kragle.
Emmet gets
so close!

The Kragle

A sticky situation

Before Emmet can put the Piece on the Kragle, Lord Business strikes back.

He takes off in his "Kraglizer." It is a giant, scary cube that can glue everything just the way he wants it.

Micro Manager

Lord Business
releases a swarm of Micro
Managers to rebuild Bricksburg.
The Micro Managers catch the
people and put them in place so
Lord Business can glue them all!

Creative ambush

Wyldstyle tells everyone that they must use their imaginations to defeat Lord Business.

The people build lots of awesome vehicles and weapons! A garbage truck is transformed into a flying Trash Chomper.

Mouth snaps open to gobble Micro Manager

Cone gun

Flick missiles

An ice-cream truck is rebuilt
into an incredible flying machine.
It has a huge ice-cream cone gun.
The battle is on!

Emmet to the rescue!

Emmet is inspired by seeing ordinary people being creative. They are all special!

Emmet builds a giant robot to fight back against the Kraglizer.

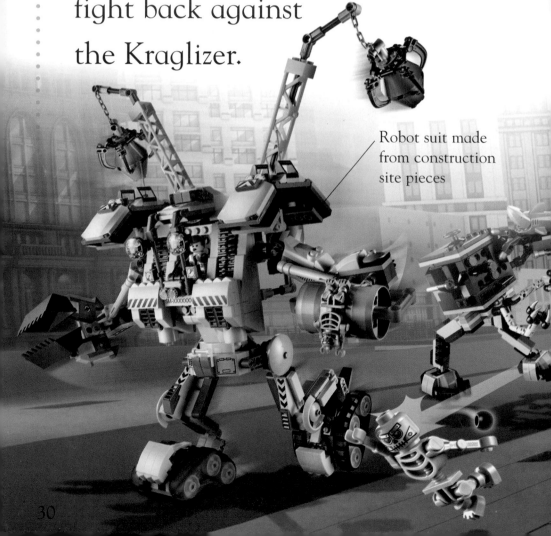

Robot suit made from construction site pieces

Emmet's friends clear the way
for him to get inside the Kraglizer.
Emmet tells Lord Business
that he is the only person who
can end this sticky situation.
He is special, too!

Lord Business finally puts
the Piece on the Kragle.
The universe is saved! Hooray!

Quiz

1. Where does Emmet live?

2. What is this object called?

3. Who lives in Cloud Cuckoo Land?

4. Who attached a tracking device to Emmet's leg?

5. What is this machine called?

1. Bricksburg, 2. The Piece of Resistance, 3. Unikitty, 4. Bad Cop, 5. A Micro Manager